Ebony
and Scarlet

EBONY AND SCARLET

Poems of the Anglo-Zulu War

Harry Turner

Pen & Sword
MILITARY

First published in Great Britain by
PEN AND SWORD MILITARY
an imprint of
Pen and Sword Books Ltd
47 Church Street
Barnsley
South Yorkshire S70 2AS

ISBN 978 1 47386 302 6

Printed and bound in England by
CPI Group (UK) Ltd, Croydon, CR0 4YY

Typeset in Palatino by CHIC GRAPHICS

Pen & Sword Books Ltd incorporates the imprints of
Pen & Sword Archaeology, Atlas, Aviation, Battleground, Discovery,
Family History, History, Maritime, Military, Naval, Politics, Railways,
Select, Social History, Transport, True Crime, Claymore Press,
Frontline Books, Leo Cooper, Praetorian Press, Remember When,
Seaforth Publishing and Wharncliffe.

For a complete list of Pen and Sword titles please contact
Pen and Sword Books Limited
47 Church Street, Barnsley, South Yorkshire, S70 2AS, England
E-mail: enquiries@pen-and-sword.co.uk
Website: www.pen-and-sword.co.uk

Contents

For Jamie Wilson,
firm friend and wise counsel

Acknowledgements

The Washing of the Spears by Donald R. Morris (Jonathan Cape, London, 1966)

Zulu Rising by Ian Knight (Macmillan, London 2010)

The Anatomy of the Zulu Army by Ian Knight (Macmillan, London 2004)

Zulu by Saul David (Viking Books, London 2004)

The Curling Letters by Adrian Greaves & Brian Best (Pen & Sword , Barnsley, South Yorkshire 2001)

Warrior Race by Lawrence James (Little Brown & Co., London 2001)

Zulu Hart, A Novel by Saul David (Hodder and Stoughton, London 2009)

Ghosts of Empire by Kwasi Kwarteng (Bloomsbury, London 2011)

Disraeli by Robert Blake (Eyre & Spottiswood, London 1966)

Redcoat by Richard Holmes (Harper Collins, London 2005)

Rorke's Drift by James W. Bancroft (Jonathan Ball, Johannesburg 1989)

Introduction

The nineteenth century saw the British Army engaged in a series of monumental engagements around the globe. In almost every continent the Redcoats of our soldiers seemed in perpetual action against enemies of the Crown.

After giving Napoleon Bonaparte a bloody nose in the Peninsular War across Spain and Portugal we were obliged to finish the job in 1815 at the Battle of Waterloo.

1854 saw our soldiers wrapped in a titanic struggle with the Russians in the Crimean War.

Just three years later in the jewel of the Empire's Crown, India, British Redcoats were again in bloody conflict during the Indian mutiny.

The 1879 Anglo-Zulu war in South Africa was brief but equally bloody and one which many historians believe was unnecessary and mistaken.

Prime Minister Benjamin Disraeli expressed shock and disbelief that a group of half-naked, apparent savages, armed only with spears could give the British Redcoats such a mauling before they were finally overcome.

In fact King Cetshwayo's Zulus were a superb, disciplined and courageous people, savage perhaps, but with their own code of honour and capable of showing remarkable tactical skill and endurance.

This short war in South Africa was the stuff of legend, brimful of dash and daring, illuminated by extraordinary characters on both sides – from the great Zulu Generals to Queen Victoria's great nephew the Prince Imperial (Napoleon III's son) who was sent out to join the British troops in their ferocious struggle against the Zulu Impis.

The war was started without any sanction from the British Government, by our men "on the spot" so to speak, led by Sir Henry Bartle Frere whose statue, surprisingly, still stands in London's Embankment Gardens.

Although the British arrived in the Cape in 1806, they were much resented by the Afrikaner settlers. Thousands of Boer families withdrew from their farms in which they had toiled for years before the British arrived, packed their possessions onto ox-carts and set off into the unknown.

As this book is primarily, if not exclusively, about the relationship between the British and the Zulus I have chosen not to dwell upon the history of the Boers in Africa - their story, also in its way remarkable, is fuel for a separate book altogether.

There have been two excellent cinema epics about the Anglo-Zulu war – "Zulu Dawn" which was about the fateful Battle of Isandlwana and of course "Zulu" which covered the siege of Rorke's Drift and which gave Michael Caine his first starring role.

In spite of having seen both these films many times they cannot even remotely match the experience and privilege I had of a one-to-one, three hour conversation with the late David Rattray on the site of Rorke's Drift in 2006.

David's mesmerising words and fabulous knowledge of the Battle were worth a million movie moments.

While I have chosen to re-tell the story of the Anglo-Zulu war in verse I am indebted to a number of authors whose scholarly work on the subject has furnished me with a treasury of information and deep historical insight. The most prominent being the brilliant Ian Knight, the equally dazzling Saul David and the extraordinary New Yorker, Donald R. Morris.

Acknowledgements to these men and their work, along with others, are listed in the following pages.

Harry Turner
Weybridge, Surrey, 2016

The Poems

1

"UHLALANKHOSI" (THE TREE OF KINGS)

Beneath the azure helmet of the sky
And a piercing orange sun,
Flit a million tiny insects
Whose lives have just begun.

The landscape is majestic
But brittle and bone dry,
And from a distant thorn bush
You can hear a leopard sigh.

The first dawn mist has melted
And the plains are bathed in light,
Showing every undulation
Almost shadowless and bright.

Upon this vast arena
Human figures can be seen,
They cloak the slopes in thousands
Bible-black against the green.

For this is Zulu country
And has been since time began
For warrior and farmer
And for woman, child and man.

Between the winding swathes of grass
Horned cattle slowly graze,
And tiny lads with painted sticks
Their bovine herds appraise.

Close by are huts of mud and straw
All nestled in the hill,
Outside squat Zulu women
Whose voices pipe and trill.

The menfolk are approaching
Back from an early hunt,
While in the village lean hounds bark
And bristled, porkers grunt.

The hunt has been successful
And tonight there'll be a feast,
Washed down with millet beer in cups
To toast the slaughtered beast.

Much later in the morning
As the sun has reached its peak,
Where the blades of whispering grasses
Fringe an ancient long-dry creek.

A clutch of youthful warriors
Bodies glistening with sweat
Gather round a gnarled black thorn tree
Like old comrades who've just met.

Theirs is a timeless ritual,
Paying homage to the dead
Whose ghostly spirits have been caught
On the thorns above their heads.

Though the men stand there in silence
As their forebears they recall
In thoughts and prayers devoutly
Each man, no less stands tall.

Among these stalwart warrior boys
Are some of tender years,
Who will pass the test of manhood
By the washing of their spears *

They are the mightiest tribe in Africa
A proud and fiercesome race
A mixture quite astonishing
Of savagery and grace.

They all revere the ritual
And conscious of their past,
Accept that even youthfulness
Will not forever last.

Their battle hardened discipline
Achieved by ruthless drill
Is matched by awesome courage
And the huntsman's lethal skill.

These are the "naked savages"
Who the British have to face,
As the Empire seeks expansion
For its Queen – and God's good grace.

---

* A rite of adult passage for a young Zulu who had to kill a wild animal or even an enemy
- thus "washing" his spear in blood.

2

REDCOATS

Salute the British soldier
In his tunic of bright red
For he is strong in heart and limb
And will follow where he's led.

Recruited from the cities' poor
From workhouse, slum or prison,
It's from these stark beginnings then,
An army has arisen.

It matters not a jot of course
Whether he is keen or willing
But his life will change forever now
As he takes the old Queen's shilling.

He'll see a lot of action too
When many miles from home,
In tropic heat and freezing cold
Through mud and frost and loam.

His stamina is amazing
When all is said and done
He'll wear that thick red jacket too,
Under a blazing sun.

The rations they will feed him on
Would scarcely fill a sparrow,
But he's hard and small and sinewy
His hips are lean and narrow.

He's drilled and marched from daylight
To the setting of the sun
He's handy with a bayonet
And useful with a gun.

He's travelled on a troopship
Across oceans that are vast,
And if he's insubordinate
He'll be flogged before the mast.

But now he's here in Africa
In a canvas-tented camp
Where the days are hot as Hadés
And the nights are cool and damp.

Around him are black faces
He has never seen before
His mother said, when he was young
"You can never trust a Moor".

He sometimes asks his sergeant
"What's the purpose of this trip?"
The grizzled man scowls down at him
Shouts "button up your lip!"

He occasionally sees officers
They are like a race apart,
When mounted high on horseback
They look very much the part.

The subalterns are younger men
Most born of noble blood
But they will lead their men in war
Through jungle swamps and mud.

Perhaps one night while sitting
By the campfire's rosy glow
A friendly corporal will talk
His accent soft and low.

He will whisper of the Zulus
These mysterious savage men
Of how each single one 'tis said
Has the actual strength of ten!

"This cannot be!" a trooper cries
As his eyes grow even bigger,
"Surely no soldier of the Queen -
Can be bested by a nigger".

The corporal, a veteran
Sucks hard upon his pipe
He doesn't answer straightaway
As he's a thoughtful type.

"You lads may mock them all you like"
Says the corporal with a frown,
As he puts his thumb up on his pipe
To tamp the baccy down.

"Now listen hard" he says to them
"To every word I utter
A Zulu spear will skewer you
Just like a knife through butter"

"I've seen the Zulu close-up
He don't have a word for fear
And his rations would surprise you
He drinks milky curds and beer"

"Underestimate your Zulu
And you will be a fool,
So respect him as an equal
That is the golden rule"

"He may be black and barefoot
But he's as swift as a gazelle
He can run across the roughest ground
And then fight like bloody hell"

"So no more idle chatter lads
Let's pause and take a breath,
Just don't forget the things I've said
The price could be – your death."

Next day as dawn is breaking
Painting red streaks in the sky
This is the "Shepherd's Warning"
And a hint that men may die.

3

THE RAINBOW NATION

The British High Commissioner
Sir Henry Bartle Frere
Was a man who'd had a great success
In his glittering career.

Imperialist to his fingertips
Both disciplined and stern
He felt that here in Africa
Still more plaudits he might earn.

His instincts were expansionist
When he assumed his post,
As Victoria's representative
And her Imperial host.

Now the Mzinyathi river
Was the natural divide
Between Britain and the Zulus
Who all lived the other side.

White settlers too were thinly spread
Along the river's arm,
Country folk and missionaries
Who came to preach or farm.

Most Africans around the Cape
Had lived in peace for years
While British rule they found benign
The Zulus stoked their fears.

11

There had been low-key conflicts
Between local native groups,
But nothing that would cause alarm
Or disturb the British troops.

Across the Mzinyathi
The Zulu kingdom thrived
Living proof if such were needed
That the strongest now survived.

Though divided by the river
Both sides were keen to trade
And with leather hides or cattle
Many bargains would be made.

The British found acceptable
What they called this "trade in trifles",
That is until a foolish white
Sold the Zulus English rifles.

When Sir Henry first was told of this
As he dined on chicken curry
He frowned and shrugged and shook his head
'Twas his only sign of worry.

Among the many missionaries
Who were there to preach and pray,
Were those who wanted Zululand
To adopt the Christian way.

But the Zulus were indifferent
To the teachings from the Bible
They preferred their own traditions
Which were primitive and tribal.

When Bishop John Colenso
One evening over dinner
Told Sir Henry it was his intent
To convert each Zulu sinner –

– Sir Henry took a swig of port,
Glared at the pious priest,
He deemed it was damn foolish
And a waste of time at least.

The overarching problem
As Sir Henry now explained,
Was increasing British territory
To that already gained.

"This country may be huge" he said
"But pasture land is tight
So we'll have to move the Zulus on
And if necessary fight."

The Bishop was astounded,
His hand trembled as he spoke,
Perhaps it was Sir Henry's way
Of making a bad joke.

"But surely sir", the Bishop said
"The Zulus don't want war
Their wish to farm and live in peace
Lies at their very core."

At this Sir Henry's face grew red
"You are mistaken sir –
The Zulu has a lust for blood
He's a savage, violent cur."

"I further make it plain to you –
This country is a mess
A jigsaw sir, of many parts
And one I'll soon redress."

Another thing that rankled
With Sir Henry Bartle Frere
Was the survey he'd commissioned *
Somewhat earlier in the year.

Instead of its conclusion
Being favourable to the British,
It found instead for Zululand
Which made Sir Henry skittish.

But Sir Henry was not thwarted
And continued to insist
That his plans for more expansion
No naked savage could resist.

He knew deep down, in the very depths
Of his imperial soul
That only by the force of arms
Could he achieve his goal.

After dining with the Bishop
Who he found a holy bore,
He went to bed determined now
To prosecute a war.

---

* The Boundary Commission met at Rorke's Drift in March 1878 and after many weeks concluded that the entire Blood River area was part of the Zulu Kingdom.

But how was he to do this?
Pull off this daring ruse?
He'd send demands to Zululand
That they'd certainly refuse.

He'd not inform his government
Or Disraeli back at home
He'd simply brief his officers
And act virtually alone.

He would summon to his presence
The officer commanding
And his words to General Thesiger *
Were persuasive and demanding.

---

* Frederic Augustus Thesiger, who later became Lord Chelmsford.

4

CETSHWAYO

His limbs are sheathed in muscle
On his head a beaded ring,
With a leopard pelt around his hips
He looks every inch a King.

Before him on the hard-stamped ground
Are a dozen of his sons
All fully blooded warriors
Carrying spears and shields and guns.

Bodies slick with anointed oils
They stand there shoulder-tight,
And gleam like jet-black mirrors
In the unforgiving light.

They are the young lieutenants
In the service of their King –
Against their shields they strike their spears
With a bass profundo ring.

They all stand tall in the Royal Kraal
But only to add lustre
For with his Impi's* all close by –
Thirty thousand he can muster!

---

* An Impi is a Zulu Regiment.

Cetshwayo sits upon a throne
Of bamboo wood and reeds
Attended by three maidens
Who are there to serve his needs.

The generals who command here
Are all hand-picked by the King,
From ancient battles half-forgot
Great experience they bring.

More than a few have greying hairs
But all are panther-thin
Though most have not seen fifty moons
Nor lost the will to win.

Outside the Kraal, a thousand huts
All built of straw and mud
And outside each, a woman squats
Mixing milky curds with blood.

Beyond this fine domestic scene
A verdant pasture lays
Where bovine herds, big-horned and plump
All bend their heads to graze.

Boy drovers armed with pointed sticks
Run naked through the cattle,
The animals move sluggishly
As their wooden neck-bells rattle.

A great arena has been cleared
On orders from the king
And the boy drovers high pitched cries
Through the crisp clear air still ring.

And now as if by magic
The arena fills with men
That human tide of hundreds
Seems to multiply by ten.

The warriors then form a line
Behind their cow-hide shields
And each, without exception now
Has a weapon that he wields.

Cetshwayo stands before his men
His sons on either side,
He gazes at the mighty throng
With dignity and pride.

"I speak today of many things
Of trickery and deceit
Of promises now broken
That lie crumbled at our feet.

The British say that we must change,
Cast off the life we lead –
Disown our old traditional ways
And to their threats pay heed

We must disband our Impi's
And repeal our Zulu laws –
Allow their priests to preach to us –
Point out our many flaws.

And all those things they ask of us
They say we must obey
It is the will, of their white Queen
And the God to whom they pray.

It has been our tradition
To deny each man a wife,
Until he is a warrior –
And reached maturity in life.

Hark how the British sneer at this
Demand we must not tarry –
– In letting those with unwashed spears
Choose who, and when, they marry.

This very land, on which we stand
And where our cattle graze
Has been in our possession now
Since very ancient days.

The rich red soil, on which we toil
From dawn to star-kissed night
May soon be taken, just to feed
The Imperial appetite.

I say to you my warriors
No quarrel do we seek
– If the British cross the river though
Our response will not be weak.

Should they set foot in Zululand
We must sharpen up our spears
And be prepared to each endure
The salt of widows' tears."

The warriors all gathered here
Like a forest of black trees,
Now start the curious humming sound
Of a swarm of honey bees.

The humming grows in volume,
Becomes a might roar
Usuthu! is the battle cry
To the heavens it will soar.

Meantime, across the river
The English now take tea,
With dainty cakes and sandwiches
Under a tall oak tree.

Sir Henry asks Lord Chelmsford
To scrutinize a map
"Do you think we'll meet resistance
From this Cetshwayo chap?"

"I have no doubt", Lord Chelsmford says
"There is no cause to worry
The thing will be quite finished off
After the merest flurry."

5

ISANDLWANA
20 January 1879

The sharp edge of the mountain
Is like a sleeping sphinx,
And veering down its rock-strewn slopes
In coarse rough grass it sinks.

Beyond this craggy silhouette
Lies a donga-riddled plain
Which in its vastness is a place
That doesn't have a name.

Below at Isandlwana
The British troops make camp
And though the dew has lifted
The grasses are still damp.

They have earlier crossed the river
And are now in Zululand,
With their wagons and their canvas tents
Just exactly as was planned.

The scouts who ride ahead of them
Have seen nothing to alarm
Save a scattering of drover boys
From a native cattle farm.

Lord Chelmsford on his chestnut horse
Reins back and points his stick,
He looks every inch a General
And is dressed parade ground slick.

There is feverish activity
As the soldiers, and some scouts
Attempt to unload wagons
And mark out the clear redoubts.

But the wagons, drawn by oxen
Have been cumbersome and slow
The animals are exhausted
By the massive weight they tow.

The N.N.C.* who, with our troops
Lend help with hands and tools
Assume we'll form a Laager
Which is taught to them in schools.

But Chelmsford and his Officers
Decide against this move
Believe if we dig trenches
Our safety will improve.

But the pioneers with shovels
Strike rock not pliant earth,
So entrenching is abandoned
With a degree of caustic mirth.

Reports come back to Chelmsford
From beyond the army camp
As the tents are now erected
And are lit by candle lamp.

But the General is thinking
Before the fall of night
He must winkle out the Zulu
And engage him in a fight.

---

* N.N.C. Natal Native Contingent.

His final, clear objective
Is to penetrate the heart
Of the Kingdom of Ulundi,
He can scarcely wait to start.

Still reports of Zulu movements
To their East and to their West
From Vedettes who scan the hillside
Will now prove a vital test.

But these sightings of the Zulus
First spotted, then to vanish
Makes Lord Chelmsford quite uneasy,
As his fears he strives to banish.

At length, with consultation
He decides to split his force,
He will take just one battalion –
– And he turns around his horse.

He looks to Captain Pulleine
Who is standing at his side
And says to him "the camp is yours,
Defend it well, with pride."

And then with one battalion
Lord Chelmsford canters off
As sweating soldiers standing by
To him their caps all doff.

A league or so beyond the camp
Lord Chelmsford calls a halt,
"We'll dismount here, on higher ground
So by surprise we won't be caught."

He sends Lieutenant Berkeley Milne*
Who has a Naval telescope
To ascertain the camp they've quit
Is still peaceful, so they hope.

The jaunty sailor scans the hill
And the base camp far below,
His focus, Isandlwana,
Then he turns to let them know.

"As far as I can see my Lord
The camp is quite at peace
Perhaps I see a little smoke
From cooking fires at least –"

"Of Zulus I see nothing,
Neither assegi or spear
And I am quite convinced my Lord
We have nothing now to fear."

Much later as the Group relax
To enjoy the hillside views
A messenger comes galloping
To deliver startling news –

"Isandlwana is surrounded
By a mighty Zulu horde
Unless we go immediately
They'll be wiped out my Lord!"

---

* A Royal Navy Officer attached to Chelmsford's H.Q.

6

THE DRENCHING OF
THE SPEARS

But earlier on that very day
In the scorching midday heat
The camp at Isandlwana
Has settled down to eat.

Routines of camp life now complete
The horses fed and haltered,
Ammunition heaved from oxen-carts
And the bovine creatures watered.

Many of the soldiers here today
Are scarcely more than boys,
Its not too long ago for them
That weapons were just toys.

For some among the youngest
It's their first taste of abroad
And most are still just novices
In handling gun or sword.

The Redcoats that the soldiers wear
Are no longer crisp and neat,
And calloused feet inside old boots
Are nicknamed "plates of meat".

The sun is like a hammer
And its anvil is the camp
As the gunners struggle manfully
To place field guns on a ramp.

It's during this activity
Of bustle and routine
That high on the escarpment
A few Zulus have been seen.

Captain Pulleine who commands here
Takes note of this brief sighting
And assumes they are just skirmishers,
Not Impis bent on fighting.

With seventeen hundred men at arms
And a brace of heavy guns
He feels that they can more than match
Any number of Zulu sons.

He throws a small defensive group
Beyond his tented lines,
And the young men who provide it
Feel a tingle in their spines.

Eight hundred yards along the crest
Five yards between each man
And in the centre, both the guns
To cover the whole span.

But this deployment fails to quell
A sense of deep foreboding
As the Gunners wheel their pieces out
And go through the drill of loading.

An Officer on Paulleine's staff
Now whispers to an aide,
"We're not here to face schoolgirls
I'm very much afraid –

– We ought to form a Laager
The classical defence"
But Paulleine doesn't listen
To this tactical sound sense.

A mile or two beyond the camp
There are various Zulu sightings
But it's still unclear if they still fear
The prospect of real fighting.

While on the North-East plateau
Another small patrol
Unexpectedly discovers
They have stumbled on their goal.

The vision in the valley
From their location on the hill
Initially sends through the group
A nervous, jangling thrill.

Then fear wells up inside each man
And strikes him like a gong
For the Zulus in the valley are –
– At least twenty thousand strong.

This vast horde of black warriors
Have been hidden in the valley
Waiting patiently in silence
For their Generals' call to rally.

Close packed they crouch behind their shields
All bodies slick with oil,
Their spear shafts standing sentinel
In the valleys soft moist soil.

High on hill, a mile away
An ancient General* stands
He turns his face to the valley
And raises both his hands.

This is a signal to his men,
The multitude below,
He knows that each and everyone
Will be keen to strike a blow.

Then thousands rise as if one man
All Impis of the King
As sunlight now illuminates
Each warrior's bead head-ring.

The warriors move with swiftness
As they cross the valley's track
With cowhide shields held shoulder high
Each man poised now to attack.

Their discipline is faultless
Like black-faced Grenadiers
They break into a loping run
With their fiercesome stabbing spears.

The wide horns of the buffalo
Is the shape the warriors take
And the pounding of their naked feet
Makes the earth beneath them shake.

---

* The Venerable Chieftain Ntshingwayo Ka Mahole Khoza.

The frontline of the British troops
Is now within their sight,
As the Zulus begin charging
From the left and from the right.

But the British troops are ready
And they form up in two lines
With the front rank kneeling steady
As they've done since ancient times.

An Officer with a monocle
Now gives the order "FIRE",
Then the second rank moves forward
As the kneeling rank retire.

They smartly reload rifles
Fire another hail of lead,
Which scythes into the Zulu horde,
At least a dozen cut down – DEAD.

Dense clouds of smoke from rifle fire
Obscure the Redcoats' view
But as it lifts it soon reveals
More Zulus charging through.

They leap like nimble antelopes
Over those who have been slain
And closing ranks with spears held high
Prepare to charge again.

The sweating Redcoats still stand firm
And adjust their rifle sights.
It's "mark your targets, fire at will"
In this most bloody fight.

Volley follows volley now
As the field guns buck and thunder,
Each recoil gouging sods of earth
And their axles sinking under.

The Zulu General on the hill
Now signals with a spear
And both "horns" of the "buffalo"
From left and right appear.

Drawing closer, ever closer
Come the Zulus at a run
From every throat a battle cry
Spear points glinting in the sun.

It's clear now to the British
They cannot stem the flow –
– Of the massed ranks of the Zulus,
– And ammunitions getting low.

Though some Redcoats have fixed bayonets
And maintained desultory fire,
The two front lines now turn about
As the bugle plays "RETIRE".

They scramble to their tented lines
In the shadow of the hill,
But the Zulus are among them now
To slash and hack and kill.

The camp is just a swarming mass
Of scarlet and jet black
And although they are outnumbered
No soldier turns his back.

It's hand to hand and head to head
With bayonet and spear
But the "two horns of the buffalo"
Have now sealed off the rear.

Though the Redcoats fight like demons
They're cut down like sheaves of wheat
And when they fall, they're speared again
As they lay at comrades' feet.

The British fight most valiantly
All diehards to the end,
They stand in pools of their own blood
Each regiment to defend.

A few escape the Zulu wrath,
Some scramble for a horse
But most are speared before they reach
The surging river's course.

Two Officers* of equal rank
Seize the colours of the Queen,
It must be saved from savage hands
Many battles has it seen.

But 'ere they reach the river bank
Both men are cut down dead
And the colour slides from lifeless hands
Close to the river bed.

But mercifully it floats away
On the swiftly running water,
While on the banks a Zulu throng
Show man or beast no quarter.

---

* Lieutenants Coghill and Melville

The British camp is burning bright
With a surge of smoke and flame
And wounded men are groaning –
– Some call their mother's name.

The Zulus are triumphant now
With their systematic slaughter,
As a dying Redcoat by the tents
Begs for a drink of water.

The killing is all finished now
Around each burning tent
And Zulus in red tunics
To high spirits now give vent.

Plumed clouds obscure the mountain peak
Stained purple by the sun,
Not far away hyenas crouch
Now the killing has been done.

~ o ~ o ~ o ~

When Chelmsford and his entourage
Arrive upon the scene
Some hours have passed since fighting ceased
– And it's eerily serene.

The General, now grim visaged
Views the corpses of his boys
Their bellies have been ripped open
Like long discarded toys.

This Zulu act of butchery
Is not what it seems to be
As these cuts are quite deliberate,
So each spirit can be free.

Lord Chelmsford shakes a weary head
His face now etched with grief
The carnage on the battlefield
Is quite beyond belief.

He dismounts slowly from his horse
Draws in a long deep breath
But the air inhaled is tainted now
With the sickening stench of death.*

---

* British Force – 67 Officers, 1,707 men; casualties 52 Officers, 1, 306 men
  Zulu Impis – 25,000 warriors; casualties 2,500 (estimate)

7

WINDSOR CASTLE
England

The fortress Windsor Castle
Broods stone grey above the river,
As a horse drawn coach by the iron gates
A lone passenger delivers.

The gentleman alighting
Is a sallow looking fellow
With a black coat and a top hat
And a waistcoat of bright yellow.

A servant in blue livery
Shows the gentleman inside,
They ascend a sweeping staircase
That is majestic, steep and wide.

Along a mirrored corridor
To a pair of double doors
Where another servant now appears
And for a moment all three pause.

The doors are then flung open
To reveal a huge salon
And the sallow gent adjusts his tie
Before moving slowly on.

It's a carpet now on which he treads
Of Royal Blue and Red,
As chandeliers of fine cut glass
Light the curls upon his head.

There seated in a high-backed chair
Is his Sovereign the Queen,
He makes a courtly bow to her
The deepest yet she's seen.

The Queen is small and plump and round
With her hands held in her lap
And on her hair, which is pulled back
Is a tiny, lacey cap.

"Prime Minister", the Sovereign says
"I can't believe my ears
This dreadful news from Africa
Is the stuff of widow's tears".

"A thousand British soldiers slain!
All in a single day
By naked savages it seems
For their souls we now must pray."

Disraeli, for it is he,
Emits a heavy sigh,
"It grieves me too, your Majesty
That such brave men should die".

"I am assured your Majesty
By dispatch I've just received
That reinforcements have been sent
And Chelmsford's men relieved."

"I'm certain that our soldiers,
Stout-hearted men and true,
Will overcome these Zulus
And eventually win through".

The Queen's face is a mask of stone
Her voice as cold as night.
"Prime Minister" she says briefly
"I hope this time you're right".

8

THE PRINCE IMPERIAL
1870

He was the Prince Imperial
A headstrong son of France
Who came to dwell in England
His lifestyle to advance.

Although a bloodline Bonaparte
He really loved the British,
He spent his youth in Roistering
And society found him skittish.

He spent useful time at Woolwich
To lean the art of Gunnery
If his mother* had foreseen his fate
She would have surely joined a nunnery.

For the youth was quite ambitious
And he yearned to be a soldier
To wear the smartest uniforms –
Gold rank upon his shoulder.

But his take on English history
Was at variance with his hosts,
Although resident in England
He conjured up old ghosts –

---

* His mother was the Empress Eugenie who ended up living in Farnborough, Hampshire.

– Of Frenchmen in that battle
On the field of Waterloo
The One Napoleon won of course
"Oh surely that you knew!".

But in spite of this confusion
Where his friends said he was "barmy",
He genuinely respected
The"splendid"British Army.

He dearly loved his mother –
The Empress of Belle France
But she too fled to England
From the Prussians* fierce advance.

But the dashing Prince Imperial
Learned to fence and shoot and ride
He even mastered cricket
Which he played with robust pride.

Though bumptious and impulsive
He had no official role,
And in the general scheme of things
He lacked a clear-cut goal.

He was a skilful horseman
And handy with a sabre
But no appointment in the army came
In spite of all his labour.

When news arrived in England
Of that "dreadful Zulu war"
He was hot to trot with his English chums –
Help staunch this running sore.

---

* After defeat by the Prussians, the second French Empire was extinguished

Queen Victoria, who liked him
But was anxious to protect
Asked Disraeli now, to take a hand
For the Prince – a role select –

Perhaps behind the fighting troops
Not in the harsh front line,
A spectator or observer
Seemed indubitably fine.

But dispatches from South Africa
Contained news we scarce could garner,
Of the massacre of British troops
On the slopes of Isandlwana.

The young Prince begged permission
"Please let me go and fight"
But Queen Victoria was firm
"Your duties should be light".

He pressed his suit still further,
Wrote strong persuasive letters
But would he actually toe the line
And heed counsel from his betters?

Disraeli was uncomfortable
He called it "injudicious",
To send the Prince to Zululand
Where exposure would be vicious.

The Duke of Cambridge disagreed
And whispered to the Queen,
"The Prince" he said "would be quite safe"
And refusal would be mean –

The Prince himself showed cunning now
As he strained to get his way
He even won Mama's support
When Eugenie joined the fray.

"If the Prince is just a spectator
This will serve him very well
He may wear a fancy uniform
But see naught of shot and shell".

There was another motive too
Which would further his advance
And realise his long held dream
To reclaim the throne of France.

Victoria relented
Most unusual to be sure
Disraeli shrugged and left the room
And quietly closed the door.

So thus it was that with dispatch
Prince Louis sailed away
To Africa's far distant shores
His spirits bright and gay.

Lord Chelmsford who commanded here
Now had in his charge
The ebullient young Frenchman
Whose ambition still loomed large.

The Prince was quite delighted
To be appointed A.D.C.*
His skill at sketching maps as well
Was there for all to see.

---

* Aide-de-Camp. A military officer acting as a personal assistant to a senior officer.

But Chelmsford was a General
With little time to spare
To mollycoddle Louis
Napoleon's errant heir.

Young Louis was ecstatic now
As he gloried in camp life
He had to show his keenness
Was as sharp as any knife.

He volunteered for "everything"
Rode briskly on patrol,
Which of course he shouldn't have
'Twas no part of his role.

He longed to meet some Zulus
And engage them in a fight
His commonsense was now quite lost –
– In a transport of delight.

From the aptly titled "Wolf's Lair Camp"
He went foraging and scouting
Treating every single dangerous trip
Like a harmless Hyde Park outing.

One fateful day, at three o'clock
The patrol stopped at a donga
It was clear that Zulus had camped here
But they were there no longer.

The Officer in Charge that day
Was Lieutenant Jahleel Carey
And with Prince Louis in his charge
The Lieutenant was quite wary.

The small patrol dismounted
And knee-haltered all their steeds,
To answer some of nature's calls
By the swishing foot-high reeds.

A loyal native with the group,
A keen observant scout
Found a campfire of warm ashes –
– Only recently gone out.

"It's time to move" said Carey
His face now creased with worry
But Louis, pouting like a child
Cried "what on earth's the hurry?"

The Prince's words froze on his lips
As behind them came a volley –
– A fusillade of crashing shots
To punctuate his folly.

Their horses, haltered, but close by
Began to spook and rear
And Carey, desperate, yelled "MOUNT"
His voice now charged with fear.

As the scattered group re-saddled
More musket shots rang out
And from behind the bushes
Came a savage, chilling shout –

– USUTHU! USUTHU!
A Zulu warrior's cry
High-pitched and full of menace
As it ripped up to the sky.

Young Louis' horse was "Percy"
A truly splendid mount
A reliable if lively one
On which the Prince could count.

But as Louis tried to mount his horse
With confusion all around,
His left foot missed the stirrup
And he stumbled to the ground.

He'd lost his sword in falling
But he pulled his pistol out
Then the Zulus were upon him
With a loud triumphant shout.

As they hacked at him and speared him
He showed no signs of fright
Just a young boy full of courage
Who'd put up a noble fight.

But the odds were clean against him
Though he'd given them his best,
And they plunged their spears deep into him
Through his belly and his chest.

And thus the Prince Imperial died
In the service of the Crown
But those who were to guard him *
In shame would soon all drown.

---

* Of all those supposed to "protect" Prince Louis, the man who took most of the blame
was the unfortunate Lieutenant Carey. Four years later he died in Bombay.

49

9

RORKE'S DRIFT
22 January 1879

Major Spalding who commands here
At this former Trading Post
Has a small but compact group of men
Two hundred at the most.

There have been Zulu movements
Reported on that morning
But he's uncertain of how seriously
He should take this early warning.

He's been promised reinforcements
To bolster up his men,
But they have not arrived yet
And it's past the hour of ten.

He decides to go and find them
But sees no need to hurry,
He calls for his horse and mounts it –
Showing not a trace of worry.

He turns to young Lieutenant Chard
Who is an Engineer
"I'm leaving you in charge"he says
"You have no need to fear."

"As nothing's going to happen here
Of that I'm pretty sure,
If anything, my dear old chap
You'll find it quite a bore."

Re-assured by Major Spalding,
Chard feels he can relax,
Rorke's Drift is most unlikely now
To be facing more attacks.

But by the early afternoon
Comes a message to the station
Of the massacre of British troops
By the savage Zulu nation.

Isandlwana has been taken
Its entire contingent slain
And several Impis are approaching
From the hills above the plain.

Chard turns now to a colleague,
A fellow Engineer
And out of earshot of his Sergeants
Whispers softly in his ear.

"We are the only Officers
Left in this cursed place
We'll have to re-enforce it –
And at a brisk old pace."

His comrade, name of Bromhead,
A whiskery young man
Knows both hospital and storehouse
They must protect – as best they can.

Inside the makeshift hospital
Are several wounded men
And in each space designed for three
Is crammed a crowd of ten.

Outside there is a frenzy
As defences are prepared –
With biscuit boxes, mealie bags,
There's no time to be scared.

The soldiers form a thin red line
By the piled-up mealie sacks
As two wagons are upended
To protect their sweating backs.

Ammunition is distributed,
All they have to do is wait,
Each man alone now with his thoughts
To contemplate his fate.

Lieutenant Bromhead licks his lips,
Slides his pistol from its holster,
As Chard, beside him does the same
As morale they try to bolster.

Their Colour-Sergeant* marches up
Salutes, parade-ground smart
This paragon of discipline
Is the master of his art.

"They'll come to us in swarms" he says
"But we'll be good and ready,
Don't worry Sir, I'll get a grip
And keep our lads all steady."

A Corporal of the Twenty Fourth**
Who forms part of the line
Feels a thrill of expectation
Running up and down his spine.

---

* Colour-Sergeant Bourne
** 2/24th Warwickshire Regiment

He turns towards a trooper
A Welshman, name of Jones,
Whose whole body is vibrating
Like a sack of loose old bones.

"Don't worry mate" the Corporal says
"We got guns and they got spears
And though its sweat that we might shed
For them it's blood and tears."

"I hope to God" the Welshman sighs
"That we will give him thanks"
The Colour-Sergeant passing by –
– Says "steady in the ranks".

High on the slopes, above the Drift
A puff of smoke appears,
It's followed by a rifle shot
Which echoes in men's ears.

The Colour-Sergeant shields his eyes
As he stares up at the sun
"No Zulu spear can make that sound –
Those devils have a gun"–

– "Or more than one "he whispers now
His voice is but a croak
– "Can't see a single Zulu yet –
So take aim at the smoke"–

'Tis then by some strange conjuring trick
Or dark Promethean spell,
The Zulu warriors appear
Like demons hot from hell.

The first wave is resisted
By the Redcoats withering fire
But thousands more come swarming
It seems they will not tire.

Closer still yet closer
Till men can smell their breath,
It's hand to hand and head to head
A battle to the death.

The Redcoats have to pull right back
To their mealie-bag redoubt.
"They are coming at our flanks as well!"
Is the Colour-Sergeant's shout.

Inside the whitewashed hospital
Through each broken window pane
The wounded men fire several shots,
Re-load and fire again.

It seems that they'll be overwhelmed
As the odds are far too great
Four thousand Zulu warriors now
Will surely seal their fate.

But the soldiers and the wounded
Are made of sterner stuff
All at their very fighting best
When the going now gets tough.

The thatched roof of the hospital
Explodes in orange flame
And the next job of the Redcoats
Is to save the sick and lame.

They scramble through the windows
Some comrades on their backs
While the Zulus in a frenzy
Re-double their attacks.

The tinder-dry old roof beams
All sag and then collapse,
With smoke and sparks and shooting flames
Each room a hot death trap.

The foreground of the Mission House
Is thick with Zulu dead
Some leap across the bodies
Until shot clean through the head.

From seven until midnight
The Zulus still attack
But these raids are intermittent now
And the British will not crack.

In darkness now, with heavy cloud
To mask the feeble moon
But flames - bright from the hospital
Will the bloody scene illume.

Thus through the night, by this bright light
The Redcoats all stand steady
And every man does what he can
To make sure he's good and ready.

The action now is skirmishing
There are no more attacks
The firepower of the Redcoats show –
– Just what the Zulu lacks.

At dawn the sun is rising
And the sky is painted red
In the foreground of the Mission House
Are the piles of Zulu dead.

We have scored a noble victory
Against overwhelming odds
And it's evident the Zulu hordes
Have been deserted by their Gods.

At eight o'clock, Lord Chelmsford
With his depleted central column
Comes riding to the Mission House
His expression dark and solemn.

But the rout at Isandlwana
For all its shame and noise
Has clearly been avenged now
By the valiant British boys.

The Rorke's Drift men are heroes
They've fought with iron will
But for Cetshwayo's Impis
It is a bitter pill.

A trooper kneeling by the dead
Runs his fingers through his hair
And in earshot of Lord Chelmsford
Sings out a Latin* prayer.

---

* Laudate Omnes Gentes
  Laudate Dominum
  (All peoples praise the Lord)

10

AFTERMATH

Has British pride been thus restored?
Is the Zulu war now won?
Will the blood-drenched fields of Africa
Now bleach white under the sun?

Nay, twice* before this story ends
The British will retreat
And swallow like harsh medicine
The sour taste of defeat.

Lord Chelmsford is most anxious
To reinforce his troops
With discipline and extra strength
To smash all Zulu groups.

A British force of mounted men
Suffer a dreadful rout,
With losses of both men and mounts
Before they can break out.

Now flushed with these achievements
Against British man and horse,
The Zulu Generals clearly think
They've changed the battle's course.

---

* Nitombe (Meyer's Drift), 12 March 1879
   Hlobane, 28 March 1879

But Zulu losses have been great
In blood and men and treasure
It's hard for Cetshwayo now
To get a steady measure –

– On just how weakened he's become
And how determined are the British,
To gather up their shattered troops
And fight now to the finish.

At the Battle of Khambula
The Zulus' spears are blunted
As the plucky Redcoats demonstrate
It's the Zulu who is hunted.

Now Cetshwayo is desperate,
He wants to sue for peace,
Negotiate a settlement,
From more bloodshed be released.

~ o ~ o ~ o ~

Beneath a shading palm leaf
Sits Cetshwayo on his throne
Listening carefully to his Generals
Taking note of their grave tone.

"The soil on which we graze our herds,
Is red with Zulu blood,
Three thousand brother warriors
Lie stiffening in the mud".

These words are uttered slowly
And the King just nods his head,
He knows full well, they will also tell
Of his sons among the dead.

A warrior is selected
To run like a gazelle,
Offer peace terms to the British
And end this living hell.

Cetshwayo's instinct tells him,
That the British might "play fair"
As this land of endless beauty is,
More than big enough to share.

~ o ~ o ~ o ~

For London is aware now
Of the recent bloody losses,
And that over many British dead
Will soon be Christian crosses.

Thus Chelmsford's resolution
Is to spurn all Zulu pleas,
And with all his extra firepower
Bring Cetshwayo to his knees.

11

LONDON
1879

In drawing rooms and barbers shops
In milliners and pubs
In mansions and in cottages
And smoke-filled London clubs.

The talk is of the Zulu war
In every London street
Where on a far off continent
We endured a great defeat.

But that was Isandlwana
Some several weeks ago,
And every Englishman believes
The battles' ebb and flow.

Will surely end in triumph,
No other way conceived
If the latest news from Africa
Is now to be believed.

This patriotic fervour
That defines the British race
Is one that must be satisfied
After earlier disgrace.

Wherever troopships leave our shores
Crowds gather by the key,
To cheer our plucky soldiers on
Before they cross the sea.

They cheer and shout, hang bunting out,
Blow whistles, pipes and trumpets.
While vendors hawk hot pies and cakes
And home-made buttered crumpets.

Flags flutter in most every street
It's a good excuse to party,
And these cheers and shouts, from toffs and louts
Are unanimously hearty.

Prime Minister Disraeli
While at his cabinet table
Scans the latest news from Africa
With each eagerly awaited cable.

He knows his reputation
Is but hanging by a thread
And he dreads that each report received
May reveal more English dead.

He plans a change in leadership,
Will ask Chelmsford to stand down,
Another General will replace him
To represent the Crown.

The best that he can hope for
To heal this running sore
Is that Wolseley* as Commander
Will now prosecute the war.

~ o ~ o ~ o ~

---

* Sir Garnet Wolseley

12

NATAL
South Africa

A thousand miles from London
In a lamp-lit canvas tent
Lord Chelmsford sits with head in hands
His upper body bent.

He's seen the news from London
In each raucous tabloid sheet,
These attacks are deeply personal
Blaming him for each defeat.

His state of mind is fragile,
He feels physically unwell.
Perhaps he should resign his post,
Let those devils go to hell.

But the victory at Khambula
and the triumph of Rorke's Drift
Are just enough to quell his gloom
And give his spirit a brief lift.

Until the news he fears and dreads
Of how he'll be replaced,
The awful hand that he's been dealt
Must now at last be faced.

For Garnet Wolseley is the man,
Disraeli's Government choice
A different General it seems,
Who is quick to give a voice –

– To those who caution counsel now,
Believe the war should stop,
Assert that Cetshwayo's blood
Must never spill a drop.

But Chelmsford is determined,
He must complete his task,
He'll ignore all Wolseley's orders
And drink deep from Victory's flask.

One final push is all it needs,
One mighty battle Royal,
His climax to the Zulu war
Will be worth a century's toil.

~ o ~ o ~ o ~

13

IN A FOREIGN FIELD

On the plains of Isandlwana
And the ruins of Rorke's Drift,
Soldiers armed with shovels
Work a gruesome duty-shift.

They have come to bury comrades
In the ground on which they fell,
And the silent furnace of the day,
Is still a living hell.

For the Englishmen, still mostly boys
The work's grotesquely grim,
In the empty eyes of slaughtered men
Black flies now feed and swim.

The grass is stiff with drying blood
The hard soil painted red,
A score or more of fallen men
Lie in death without a head.

The Sergeants who supervise
Are made of sterner stuff,
But some young troopers find the work
Both nauseous and tough.

Many of the dead have been neatly stripped
And lay sprawled in birthday suits.
No coats, no belts, no hats, no socks,
No underpants or boots.

The midday heat is blistering
And some troopers pray to God
As they plunge their shovels deep,
In the gore-stained earthen sod.

The Zulu dead have been removed,
The work of several hours,
But the colour of the blood they spilled
Is just the same as ours.

At a fresh dug grave a soldier stands,
A short vigil he will keep,
His head is lowered to his chest
So his mates won't see him weep.

14

THE HOSPITAL

The Sergeant is a grizzled one,
His beard is shot with grey,
When he fought in the Crimea
A Queen's shilling was his pay.

He remembers this old conflict
When he was very young,
Of those horses who were starving,
And who ate their own warm dung.

He recalls the biting winter cold,
The oozing, sliding mud,
The hoar frost on his eyebrows,
And the freezing of his blood.

He remembers every detail,
Yes every single one.
But now he knows he's dying
Under a different sun.

It's in the heat of Africa
On a makeshift canvas bed,
That these fevered thoughts now torture him
As they swim inside his head.

The fellow standing by the bed
Has done his level best,
But he is tired, and sick of war,
In his blood-soaked surgeon's vest.

His hands are stained with crimson too
Where he's sewn the Sergeant's wound,
But there's little else that he can do
As with death he's well attuned.

The patient gasps now for a breath,
With a perforated lung,
But as he dies, his staring eyes
Look child-like, even young.

15

THE ZULU PEACE OFFERING

Cetshwayo's desperation
Grows keener by the hour,
As the British answer to his pleas
Is unambiguously sour.

Two hundred oxen, plump and sleek,
The choice pick of his herd,
And a hundred pounds of ivory
To consolidate his word.

The British brush such bribes aside,
Being set firm on their course,
To subjugate the Zulu race
By sheer superior force.

For Chelmsford, it's his Waterloo,
He cannot falter now,
The telegram he's just received
Brings sweat beads to his brow.

Does the British Government at home
Believe "Peace at any price?"
Do they think that he will drop his sword
In the twinkling of a trice?

His army has been strengthened
With the fiercesome Gatling gun,
So it's onward to Ulundi
As they march into the sun.

16

DURBAN
23 June 1879

But Wolseley fresh from England
Is keen to intervene,
Headquartered now in Durban
Far from the battle's scene.

He sends specific signals
That engagement now must cease.
Lord Chelmsford and his officers
Must accept their goal – is peace.

In the maelstrom of events here
To the Tattoo of the drums
The bruised Impis of the Zulu
Know that Nemesis now comes.

Peace offerings rejected
Inducements brushed aside
As the fate of this old nation
Will be consumed by history's tide.

Above the plains an eagle soars
The wind beneath its wings,
While lower in the tree-line hills
A painted songbird sings.

But the steady tramp of soldiers' boots
And the creak of saddle leather
Rise up to meet sweet nature's sounds
As they march o'er rock and heather.

Old soldiers tire of fighting too
They've seen blood and death and plunder,
They know full well, though war is hell
They might still be ripped asunder.

But Chelmsford on a prancing horse
Believes his plans are sound,
So sends a Colonel* out ahead
To reconnoiter ground.

"Find me a battleground" he cries
As Buller pulls away –
"Where we can smite the Zulu foe
In one last glorious day!"

---

* Lieutenant-Colonel Buller

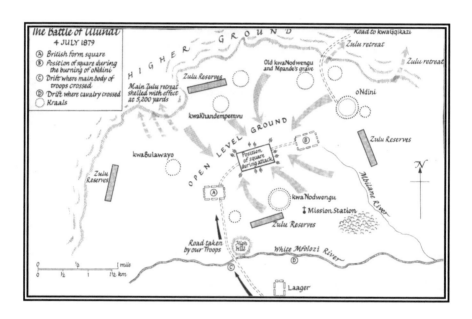

The Battle of Ulundi
4 JULY 1879

Ⓐ British form square
Ⓑ Position of square during the burning of oNdini
Ⓒ Drift where main body of troops crossed
Ⓓ Drift where cavalry crossed
◯ Kraals

HIGHER GROUND

Road to kwaGqikazi

Zulu retreat

Zulu retreat

Zulu retreat

Zulu Reserves

Old kwaNodwengu and Mpande's grave

oNdini

Main Zulu retreat shelled with effect at 5,200 yards

kwaKhandempemvu

OPEN LEVEL GROUND

Zulu Reserves

Position of square during attack

Ⓑ

kwaBulawayo

Zulu Reserves

Mbilane River

N

Ⓐ

kwaNodwengu

Mission Station

Zulu Reserves

Road taken by our Troops

High Hill

White Mfolozi River

0   ½   1 mile
0   ½   1   1½ km

Ⓒ

Ⓓ

Laager

17

THE ZULU BOY
Ulundi, 4 July 1879

Slim as a reed but supple too,
Both feet as hard as leather,
He squats to hone a spearhead
By the flattened earth and heather.

He's seen a dozen summers
But may never see another,
As he yearns to grow to manhood
And join his spear-washed brother.

The warriors of his family
Have been gone these hundred days.
But no word has reached Ulundi
Where fat bovine herds still graze.

At night he hears a Jackal howl
And a Leopards throat-thick sigh.
But the moon is weak in the darkening sky,
Reflecting in his eye.

He cannot sleep, but a vigil keep
To wait, to hope to wonder,
Will his brother live to tell his tale
Of how they stole the white man's thunder?

At dawn the low mist rises
And the heat begins to boil,
As the women crouch by earthen pots
And commence the new day's toil.

A runner slick with sweat appears
On the soft slope of the hill,
He stops breathless by the royal Kraal
And the young boy feels a thrill.

The die is cast, good news at last?
Or have their Gods deserted?
Will the runner speak of victory,
And of Zulu might asserted?

It's bustle now, around the Kraal
With stringy dogs harsh barking,
And close by the boy are younger ones
All innocently larking.

At length a greybeard elder,
A servant of the King
Appears beside Cetshwayo's Kraal,
In a beaded, feathered ring.

The news, he says in measured tones,
Brought by the sweating runner,
Is that a mighty army comes
As winter follows summer.

The white man and his devil pipes*
Are only leagues away,
A battle most stupendous now
Before the close of day.

---

* Martini Henry Rifles and Gatling machine guns

18

LAST PUSH
1879

Onward slowly move the lines
Yet forty miles from goal
Twelve thousand oxen lumbering
T'will take a heavy toll.

Ten thousand soldiers marching
No time to rest or tarry,
Lord Chelmsford knows deep in his soul
A huge burden he will carry.

He must drive on, cross silted* drifts
With guns and food and water
No power on earth save providence
Can Chelmsford's plan now alter.

Then comes the aching moment
With Ulundi clear in view
Where here the blades and guns and spears
Will prove which ones are true.

It is the British heavy guns
That spit fire and smoke and lead
As Zulu warriors are scythed down
And death among them spreads.

---

* Grass bundles were tossed into the silted riverbeds to gain purchase for the wagons.

Raw courage is on show here
Both ebony and red,
But Zulu Impis cannot crack
The British squares ahead.

And thus it is, in just four hours
The Zulus are defeated.
The Gatling guns and British pluck
Have victory repeated.

~ o ~ o ~ o ~

19

JULY 1882

Three years later
Osborne House, Isle of Wight
Queen Victoria's Residence

By a window hung with tasselled drapes,
At a polished long oak table
The Sovereign sits in sombre black
With just a hint of sable.

The table's laid with fine cut glass,
With silverware and flowers,
The dining room at Osborne House
Sits neat between its towers.

Outside the room, a garden view
Of sculpted trees and grass,
Of vine-clad bowers and Grecian urns
Through which a man could pass.

Beyond, a tinkling fountainhead
And statues lichen-covered,
Where secret places can be found
And grottoes be discovered.

The Queen turns to her special guest
Who sits on her right side,
The talk, almost in whispers
Is of the flow of history's tide.

"I only hope", the Sovereign says
"That we can live in peace,
And all the bitterness and strife
Will hence forever cease".

Cetsywayo sighs and nods his head
His hair is shot with grey
"Your Majesty", the Zulu says
"That is the only way".

Beyond the painted palace walls,
Across a distant sea,
A thousand miles away at least
By a twisted old thorn-tree,

A young boy clad in leopardskin
Is polishing his spears
They'll not be dipped in blood again
But washed clean by his tears.